Revelations from My Father

Pastor Patty Lee

Copyright © 2012 Patty Lee Ministries

All rights reserved.

ISBN:1481956574
ISBN-13: 9781481956574

Dedication

This book is gratefully dedicated to my children, my mother, my father and my husband. My mother (Mable Brownlow) who taught me how to be a woman. My father (Kerry Brownlow) who did his best for me. My children (Jasmine and Jade Lewis) who taught me the true meaning of love and provided the best days of my life. My husband…my love, my friend, my Pastor, a man of God who has loved me unconditionally. To you all I say thank you from the bottom of my heart.

Thank You Lord for Choosing Me!

CONTENTS

1	The Sower and The Seed	pg.6
2	The Napkin Is Still Folded	pg.7
3	Desire To Learn His Ways	pg.8
4	Overcomer By The Blood	pg.10
5	It Is Finished	pg.11
6	Two Are Better Than One	pg.12
7	Decree It!	pg.13
8	Do You Know the Word	pg.14
9	Doers of The Word	pg.15
10	Dominion	pg.16
11	The Power of Agreement	pg.17
12	The Cave Experience	pg.18
13	Where Are You Going	pg.19
14	The Condition of The Heart	pg.20
15	It's Up To You	pg.21
16	I Know I Can....But	pg.22
17	Spiritual Mid-Wives	pg.23
18	Wake-Up	pg.24
19	Pursue The Will of God	pg.25
20	Getting His House in Order	pg.26
21	You're Not the First	pg.27
22	Put Your Trust in God	pg.28
23	Lord, Let Your Will Be Done	pg.29
24	A Double-Minded Man	pg.30
25	What Time It Is?	pg.31
26	God Is Still in Control	pg.32
27	Help Lord, I Have A Problem!	pg.33
28	Presence of Thine Enemies	pg.34
29	Ask God To Change You	pg.35
30	Where Are The Men of God?	pg.36
31	I'll Wait!	pg.38
32	Nuggets of Truth	pg.39

1
The Sower and The Seed

Last night as I was lying in bed talking to the Lord I received a vision of a little girl planting a small seed. Every few minutes she would run outside to check on her seed to see if it was sprouting from the ground in the form of a tree yet. I saw her at least ten times going back and forth in and out of the house over several days (I knew days had passed because her clothes were different every time). The last time she went and looked she began to cry and I heard her say "Mom I still don't have apples yet" as she stood crying looking at the ground where the seed was planted. We are much like this little girl, says the Lord....we plant a seed and expect a harvest immediately. We run back and forth checking on what was planted and become angry and sad when it's not doing what we think it should. If you know anything about fruit trees, planting, sowing and harvest time you know that it takes years for an apple seed to become a full blooming apple tree (producing loads of apples)...why then do we expect the seeds sown to the Lord to produce overnight. Some of the things that you did for the Lord and seeds that you sowed to the Lord 5, 10, 15 and 20 years ago are about to produce a harvest that is full and over flowing. I hear the Lord saying "Your seeds of kindness, Your seeds of obedience, and the monetary seeds you sowed the ones that you have forgotten about are now full grown producing trees" ENJOY!

The seeds you sow today are for the harvest you'll receive tomorrow. The Lord wants the Body of Christ to know that there is a wave of favor, blessings and a harvest falling upon His people and many will hurry and try to sow to be included in this overflow but it will be given in accordance to what you sowed yesterday. Think it not strange when those placed in leadership positions begin reaping extraordinary blessings and remember that blessings and prosperity starts with the head and flows down to the body...like the oil upon the head of Aaron running down his beard and the edge of his garments.

Scripture: II Corinthians 9:6 - "But this I say He which soweth sparingly shall reap also sparingly, and he which soweth bountifully shall reap also bountifully."

2
The Napkin is Still Folded

The Napkin Is Still Folded: The Gospel of John tells us that the napkin, which was placed over the face of Jesus, was not just thrown aside like the grave clothes but it was neatly folded and placed at the head of the coffin. (John 20:7)

In the Hebrew tradition when the servant set the dinner table for his master, he made sure that it was exactly the way his master wanted it. The servant would wait, out of sight, until the master had finished eating, and he wouldn't touch the table until the master was finished. Now when his master was done he would rise from the table, wipe his fingers, his mouth, and clean his beard, and would wad up the napkin and toss it on the table. The servant would then know to clear the table because in those days, the wadded napkin meant, 'I'm done'.

I thank God today that He's not finished yet....The tomb is empty....our Savior is alive....and the napkin is still folded! He's not finished saving souls...He has the last say in your situation...It's Not Over Until God Says So and today He's saying "I'm Not Done!"

Scripture: John 20:7 "And the napkin, that was about his head, not lying with the linen clothes, but wrapped together in a place by itself."

3
Desire to Learn His Ways

If someone tells you that God said "25 people are supposed to get in line and give $1000...then it changes to 15 people giving $100 and so on" please inform them that they just told a lie on God and they will be held accountable. God does not do things in the form of an auction. Many have fell for this trick of the enemy and then wonder why what was promised never comes to pass....well it wasn't God promising you. Men and Women of God this ridiculous trickery is not of God...and it can't go on if we no longer fall for it. The bible says "My Sheep hear my voice, and I know them, and they follow me." Stop moving out of emotion and at the voice of man...wait on the voice of the Lord and desire to learn His ways!

Obedience is better than sacrifice. It's only out of obedience that we sacrifice…when God commands you to do something it's out of obedience that you do it not out of sacrifice. When we obediently move is when the hand of God is activated to move in our lives. Watch this…If someone asks you to give a thousand dollars and you get up and give it and the Lord has not spoken that to you…then you obediently moved at the command of man not God…so don't expect His hand to move because you obeyed what man was telling you to do. When God tells you to do something please know that if you do it then you are moving out of obedience and your sacrifice will be rewarded. Discern who's speaking to you and stop blaming God when you've given your last because man told you too and the Lord haven't manifested what was promised to you by man. The people of God are being tricked and then blaming it on God!

Scripture: Deuteronomy 20:30 "That thou may love the Lord thy God, and that thou may obey his voice, and that thou may cleave unto him: for he is thy life, and the length of thy days: that thou may dwell in the land which the Lord swore unto thy fathers, to Abraham, to Isaac, and to Jacob, to give them."

4
Overcomer by The Blood

I woke up this morning with my testimony on my mind and then I heard the spirit of the Lord say "And they overcame him by the blood of the Lamb and by the word of their testimony" (Rev 12:11)
So my word for you today is....Don't ever think that your testimony isn't important because according to the word of God you are made an overcomer by the blood of Jesus and by your testimony. All of the things that you've been through wasn't just for you...weren't just things you had to learn but they were things you had to experience so that you would have compassion and empathy for the people God is going to have you minister too. No...you weren't being punished, you were going through the process that produces a testimony so that God can use you.

Many times as believers we fail to realize that one of the greatest weapons we have against hell is our testimony. Your testimony makes you a threat to hell, so open your mouth and testify.

Scripture: Revelations 12:11 "And they overcame him by the blood of the Lamb, and by the word of their testimony; and they loved not their lives unto death."

5
It is Finished!

"God will allow you rest but you're never off duty!" As I was on my way to California the other day I had my eyes closed meditating on the scriptures I had just read when I heard the spirit of the Lord say "Look at the young lady next to you" (she was sitting next to me on the plane) so as I opened my eyes and glanced at her I saw cuts that covered the inner and outer parts of both of her arms. As I slowly closed my eyes back I asked the Lord "What would you like me to do?" He asked me to silently pray and as I pray she will begin to feel His presence. The Lord then showed me a vision of Jesus being whipped and the cuts that broke through His skin...for us and in our place. When I finished praying I opened my eyes and the young lady was looking at me like she was studying me...she then closed her eyes and went to sleep.

I believe, that as the young lady slept the Lord ministered to her spirit and let her know that His son took whips, was cut and tortured, and died on the cross for her pain, her hurts, and for her disappointments. When you say yes to God you're saying YES to Him using you whenever, where ever and however He chooses...was on my way to rest and still working!

Scripture: John 19:30 "When Jesus therefore had received the vinegar, he said, It is finished: and he bowed his head, and gave up his spirit."

6
Two are Better Than One

The bible says "He who finds a wife finds a good thing and obtains favor from the Lord." The bible also says "It is not good that the man should be alone; I will make him a helper fit for him."
Then God said "Therefore a man shall leave his father and his mother and hold fast to his wife, and they shall become one flesh."

What did He say about the two when they get together....I'm glad you asked! "Two are better than one, because they have a good reward for their toil. For if they fall, one will lift up his fellow. But woe to him who is alone when he falls and has not another to lift him up! Again, if two lie together, they keep warm, but how can one keep warm alone? And though a man might prevail against one who is alone, two will withstand him—a threefold cord is not quickly broken."

Scripture: Ecclesiastes 4:9-12 "Two are better than one; because they have a good reward for their labour. For if they fall, the one will lift up his fellow: but woe to him that is alone when he falleth; for he hath not another to help him up. Again, if two lie together, then they have heat: but how can one be warm alone? And if one prevail against him, two shall withstand him; and a threefold cord is not quickly broken."

7
Decree It!

As you begin to mature in the Lord, God wants you to come to the place where you decree things and speak them into existence. As a believer, you have that authority and it is scriptural for you to do so. You can take authority over problems, difficulties, circumstances and situations. You can decree that fear and confusion be gone from your life. This is part of your inheritance as a child of God. The bible says "Thou shalt also decree a thing, and it shall be established unto thee" (Job 22:28). God wants you to know today that you can speak to the mountain of sickness, fear, frustration and confusion. Whether it be spiritual, physical, mental, or financial, He has given you the authority to speak to these things and make them be moved into the sea. What will you speak and decree today?

Scripture: Job 22:28 "Thou shalt also decree a thing, and it shall be established unto thee: and the light shall shine upon thy ways."

8
Do You Know the Word?

The bible says "My people perish from a lack of knowledge." It's one thing to know your Bible, but it's another thing to KNOW the God of the Bible. When Jesus had gone forty days in the desert fasting and praying the bible says He was hungry and at a weak point...."he was faint with hunger." The Devil, the tempter had come to him. Now my question for you is this, "When does the Devil tempt you the most?" It's at your weakest moments, it's at some of the weakest points and times in your life.

How did Jesus handle this moment? He brought God into it. He quoted the Bible, God's word. Each time the Devil tried to trap Him, He would respond, "It is written!" Many people are robbed of blessings that the Bible tells us are ours in Christ Jesus simply because we don't know the word, so we never truly live in them!

Scripture: 2Timothy 3:16 "All scripture is given by inspiration of God, and is profitable for doctrine, for reproof, for correction, for instruction in righteousness."

9
Doers of The Word

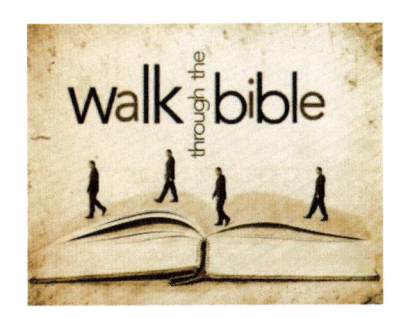

Faith is the supernatural sense that's birthed in the human heart when God's word is heard, received, believed, and acted on. The bible lets us know that believers are more than agree'ers they're doers. The plague that has infected the people of God is simply that we're calling mental assent (the agreement of the mind) a vital and living faith, but it's not believing without corresponding actions. Believers are Doers and Doers are See'ers...so we'll only see the manifestation in the doing, not the agreeing. Many people say that they believe what the bible says and they believe God's word. But if they're not living according to His principles, then they don't believe they just agree. When we believe we'll do, and when we do what we're agreeing with we'll see the power of God. It's time to be a Doer of the word.

Scripture: James 1:22 "But be you doers of the word, and not hearers only, deceiving your own selves."

10
What God Meant by Dominion

This morning I woke up with dominion on my mind and as I was making my coffee several thoughts kept running through my mind...Man has gotten things so wrong...people are trying to have dominion over people and that is not what God said. How are you going to take dominion over another born again believer? The bible says "So God created man in his own image, in the image of God created he him; male and female created he them. And God blessed them, and God said unto them, Be fruitful, and multiply, and replenish the earth, and subdue it: and have dominion over the fish of the sea, and over the fowl of the air, and over every living thing that moveth upon the earth." When God said every living thing He was not talking about your brothers and sisters in Christ. God's word tells us that it's pleasing to Him when we dwell together in unity (on one accord) so this does not mean we have the dominion or the authority to try and rule, reign, and subdue our brothers and sisters in Christ. You can't sit down what God stood up and You can't silence what God has commanded and ordained to speak. We need to get ourselves together and begin taking authority and dominion over what God said and leave everything else to the Lord!

Scripture: Luke 10:19 "Behold, I give unto you power to tread on serpents and scorpions, and over all the power of the enemy: and nothing shall by any means hurt."

11
The Power of Agreement

The place of agreement is the place of power and the place of confusion is one filled with envy and strife. Now the bible asks a question in the book of Amos "How can two walk together except they be agreed?" And in Matthew 18:19 it states "If two of you shall agree on earth as touching any thing that they shall ask, it shall be done for them..." Matthew 12:25 states, "A house divided against itself shall not stand" and Deuteronomy 32:30 declares, " One can chase a thousand, and two can put ten thousand to flight."

The Bible is replete with the fact that agreement is very important if we want to maximize our power and success and minimize strife, discord, and failure. So today I ask you "Who and what have you agreed with?" I'm hearing in the spirit "Work towards agreement and then take me at my word."

Scripture: Matthew 18:19 "Again I say to you, that if two of you agree on earth about anything that they may ask, it shall be done for them by My Father who is in heaven."

12
The Cave Experience

The caterpillar would never make the transition into the most glorious and beautiful butterfly were it not for the dark confines of it's cocoon. And you and I would never make the transition to the fresh and the new if it wasn't for our cave experiences.

Somebody is in a cave right now, but God wants you to know that this is just a temporary condition. You're in transition and much like Elijah you're coming out slinging oil, with a fresh fire, a fresh vision, a new passion, and a new sense of purpose. And the very thing that ran you into the cave is ultimately going to be responsible for pushing you to your next level. Jezebel you lose…our place of hiding has turned into our place of rest, restoration, and growth. Men and women of God don't despise your cave time….it's not a tomb it's a womb, it's not the end it's just the beginning of a brand new chapter.

Scripture: Psalm 3:3-6 "But You, O LORD, are a shield for me, My glory and the One who lifts up my head. I cried to the LORD with my voice, And He heard me from His holy hill. I lay down and slept; I awoke, for the LORD sustained me. I will not be afraid of ten thousands of people. Who have set themselves against me all around."

13
Where Are You Going?

How do you get where you're going? First, by knowing where you're going. So many of us are just wandering around clueless and refuse to stop and ask for instructions, a plan, a map, and directions from the Lord. Second, by staying in your own lane. Many of God's children are so busy looking at the direction others are going in that they're driving all over the road causing chaos and confusion...stay in your lane and keep your eyes on where you're supposed to be going. Third, slow down! If you want to make it to your destination/destiny alive then you better slow down. For everything there is a season. God never told you you'll get there overnight....there are some things you have to learn on your way. Last but not least....know when you've arrived. It may not look like you thought it would but just as Abraham did...pitch your tent and wait on the Lord! God gives us specific instructions. If you don't listen to the voice of the Lord you'll keep on going and miss out on what He had for you in the location you thought you were better than.

Scripture: Psalm 25:5 "Lead me in your truth, and teach me: for you are the God of my salvation; on you do I wait all the day."

14
The condition of the heart

This morning I'm hearing that there's some grounds that need to be plowed! The ground is your HEART and the plow is a proper relationship with God. The plow has 3 prongs or tillers on it and I'm seeing that they are the prongs of fasting, praying, and reading the Word of God. Many people don't like the plow because it digs deep into the soil of our heart and up roots stuff that is growing there and simply don't have no business in there. It up roots jealousy, envy, malice, strife. It crushes backbiting, favoritism, and cliques. It turns over hatred, self-reliance, and pride. No-one really cares for the plow because the plow disrupts complacency and it does away with mediocrity. It exposes disunity and inconsistency and it takes the comfort zone and turns it into discomfort. We, as a people don't necessarily like the plow....but God wants us to know today that there is Power after the plow.

There are people who are going to miss out on what they need from God and have been expecting from God because of the condition of their heart! God doesn't watch our lips moving He listens to what the heart is saying. What has your heart been speaking...Good or Evil, Love or Hate, Blessings or Curses...God is listening. How is the condition of your heart?

Scripture: Psalm 51:10 "Create in me a clean heart, O God; and renew a right spirit within me."

15
It's up to you!

While at school this morning I sitting and studying for a test and I had to put my notes away and begin to write what I was hearing. Question: "Who is essentially responsible for making your life better and a more positive experience?" Answer: "YOU ARE!" You are responsible for your successes, failures, and creating positive experiences in your life. We as a society tend to blame our failures on others while proudly claiming our successes as a remarkable thing that we have done. Your failures in life are not your families fault nor is it the Presidents...they're YOURS, as well as your successes. If you want a better paying job then get a better education. If you want to see a difference in your finances then do what it takes to see it (discipline and action). If you want a brighter tomorrow then start applying yourself today. You determine your tomorrow by what you do today so take responsibility and stop blaming others for what you don't have the courage to complete, the drive to achieve, and the determination to obtain. The question really isn't who our President will be for the next four years....It's who will you be! What God has for you is for you and can't nobody stop His hand but you and the decisions you make concerning your life.

Scripture: Philippians 4:13 "I can do all things through him who strengthens me."

16
I Know God Can...But!

How many times have we stood on the border of our promised land, and failed to take possession simply because we couldn't believe God was able? Every time you add a BUT to the promises of God you limit God, and disqualify yourself from His promise and from His provision.

I know God can heal, BUT.

I know God can deliver, BUT.

I know God can save, BUT.

I know God can open doors, BUT.

I know God can bring water out of a rock, BUT can He put food on my table.

I know God can, BUT.

Men and Women of God it's when you take the BUT out of the equation that you will see the manifestation of God's promises in your life...so NO MORE BUTS!

Scripture: Matthew 21:21 Jesus answered, "I assure you that if you believe and do not doubt, you will be able to do what I have done to this fig tree. And not only this, but you will even be able to say to this hill, "Get up and throw yourself in the sea,' and it will."

17
Spiritual Mid-Wives

I was very uncomfortable for most of the day yesterday and though I just wanted to lay down some where I had to keep moving. When I finally settled in for the evening I received a message that disturbed my spirit and made my stomach hurt even worse. So I called my spiritual counselor, cousin and one of my best-friends (Karen Jacobs) who talks me through everything and as she quoted scriptures I started feeling better and this morning when I opened my eyes it felt like I had given birth to something during the night. What am I trying to say...There are some spiritual Mid-wives that God has appointed to help you push...push out of your storm and right into your destiny...Push pass foolishness and right into the word of God...Push when you feel like aborting the plan and the call on your life. Men and Women of God I encourage you to ask the Lord to show you who He's appointed to tell you when to push so you can stop trying to go at it alone. The enemy wants you sitting by yourself so he can rap the cord of discouragement around that baby's neck and kill it before it even gets here but if you have a mid-wife she'll be there to flip that baby until it becomes untangled...Glory to God! My baby survived and I give God all the glory!

Believe It and Trust the Lord!

18
Wake-Up!

Life has a way of putting us to sleep, we lose our passion, We lose our vision, sometimes we get the breath knocked out of us, and things happen and we get discouraged. We walk around murmuring and complaining and treating God like some sort of Santa Claus. When this happens our faith becomes weak and there is a tendency to slip into a kind of spiritual slumber or sleep. I'm convinced that we're at a critical point in time in the spiritual realm and I believe there has been a strong spirit of slumber that has fallen upon the church world, and many believers are guilty of sleep walking through life. Oh but I hear the Lord saying "You better wake-up...while you're wandering around complaining I'm raising up Caleb's and Joshua's who will receive the promise."

The bible says "How long shall I bear with this evil congregation who complain against Me?" "Say to them, As I live says the Lord, just as you have spoken in My hearing, so I will do to you." Men and Women of God what the Lord is ministering to my spirit this morning is to watch your mouth and wake-up if your desire is to enter into the promise.

Scripture: Ephesians 5:14 "Awake, you who sleep, Arise from the dead, And Christ will give you light."

19
Pursue the will of God

You won't receive the promise without first pursuing and completing the will of God for your life...for the bible says "You have need of endurance, so that after you have done the will of God you may receive the promise" (Hebrews 10:36). When we move outside the will of God we end up in a place of bondage and that which you moved to you will be bonded too.

What is the will of God for my life? The bible says, "I beseech you therefore brethren, by the mercies of God, that you present your bodies a living sacrifice, holy, acceptable to God, which is your reasonable service. And do not be conformed to this world, but be transformed by the renewing of your mind, that you may prove what is that good and acceptable and perfect will of God" (Romans 12:1). That is the will of God for our lives...believe it and trust Him...You can't have His promises without His will!

Scripture: Galatians 3:29 ""And if ye be Christ's, then are ye Abraham's seed, and heirs according to the promise."

20
Getting His House In Order

I believe that Christ wants His Church to be unshockable, a fellowship where people can come in and say, "I'm tired, I'm beat, and I've had it. I believe people need to know that they can go to church and be loved and accepted for who they are. They need to know that they can go and find people who care more about them, than what they've done in the past. They need to know that the church is a place where people are willing to help bear their burdens. I believe that God's children need to know that they can share their problems with someone at church without worrying about the entire city finding out every word they shared. Thus far in life I've learned that most people go to the bar because that's where they feel welcomed, that's where everybody knows their name, and that's where they feel loved. God's house is a house of Love…where every soul matters and every face has a name and not just a number…In this next year God is getting His houses in order and the Church will not be in competition with the bar!

Scripture: Deuteronomy 31:6 "Be strong and of a good courage, fear not, nor be afraid of them: for the LORD your God, he it is that does go with you; he will not fail you, nor forsake you."

21
You're Not The First

As I was getting dressed this morning for Church the Lord gave me a word for His people..."Open your bibles and see that you're not the only one who has gone through what you're going through nor are you the first!" You're not the only who went through persecution...look at Jesus. You're not the only one who was left as a single parent...look at the widow of Zarephath. You're not the only one who was punished for jumping ship and saying NO to your assignment...look at Jonah. You're not the only one who ever lost everything they had, including children....Look at Job. You're not the only with a past...look at the Samaritan women. You're not the only one who was thrown in a den with crazy lions...look at Daniel. You're not the only one who has ever had issues...Look at the woman with the issue of blood. You're not the only who needed God to fight your battles...look at David.

Glory be to God Open your bibles and see that you're not the only one who has gone through what you're going through, nor are you the first...The same way God showed up for them He's about to show up for you.

Scripture: Proverbs 3:5-6 "Trust in the Lord with all your heart; lend not on your own understanding. Seek his will in all you do, and he will show you which path to take."

22

Put Your Trust in God

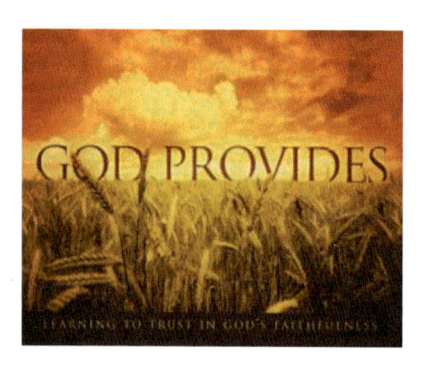

The same God that delivered Daniel from the Lion's Den is the same God that's able to deliver you...the same God that healed the woman with the issue of blood is the same God that's able to heal you....The same God that made a way in the wilderness for the children of Israel is the same God that will make a way for you...The same God that commanded Pharoh to let His people go is the same God that's commanding the enemy to free you....The same God that placed Himself in the fiery furnace with the three Hebrew boys is the same God that has placed Himself in the fire with you. We serve a God that never changes...He is the same Yesterday, Today, and Forever more! Put your trust and your faith in the only unchanging thing in this world.

Scripture: Hebrews 13:8 *"Jesus Christ the same yesterday, and today, and forever".*

23

Lord, Let Your Will Be Done

It's possible to be asking and receiving and be fat in the things of personal desires of the flesh and yet be starving to death spiritually. It's possible to gain the world, and lose your soul. It's possible to be so preoccupied with the good things that we can get from God, that we forget all about him. It's possible to lose the presence and the operation of the Holy spirit in your life, and not even know it. It's possible to have more than you've ever had, and be less than you've ever been. It's possible to be living your dream, while God's dream for you dies.

The bible says "But they lusted exceedingly in the wilderness, and tested God in the desert. And He gave them their request, but sent leanness into their soul" (Psalm 106:14). Men and Women of God understand that they got what they wanted for their flesh, but lost what they needed for their souls. Don't let this be you...before you go to God in prayer requesting things first ask Him what He desires for your life and let your response be "Your will Lord, Not mine!"

Scripture: Psalm 40:8 "I delight to do your will, O my God: yea, your law is within my heart."

24

A Double-Minded Man

The bible says "A double-minded man is unstable in all his ways" (James 1:8). In this scripture James is describing someone who is divided in his interests or loyalties, wavering, uncertain, two-faced, and half-hearted. A double-minded man is a dangerous person and if the Lord is showing you this in someone then you need to take heed to the warning.

Before examining the words that flow from our mouth we should examine the thoughts of our minds and hearts, for, as Jesus said, "Out of the abundance of the heart the mouth speaks" (Luke 6:45). We cannot always control what we hear, but we can control what we hold dear in our hearts. Each day Satan, the "prince of the power of the air" relentlessly inspires a multitude of improper thoughts. Therefore, we must "take captive every thought to make it obedient to Christ.

I've never seen a person gossip alone or a two-faced person talking to himself. So we the Body of Christ must stop helping people be double-minded the devil doesn't need our help!

Scripture: James 1:5-8 "If any of you lack wisdom, let him ask of God, that gives to all men liberally, and upbraideth not; and it shall be given him. But let him ask in faith, nothing wavering. For he that wavereth is like a wave of the sea driven with the wind and tossed. For let not that man think that he shall receive any thing of the Lord. A double minded man is unstable in all his ways.

25

Do You Know What Time It Is?

As you sit and reflect on the previous year and all of those who started out with you in the new year and those that left you somewhere along the way you'll come to realization that they weren't concerned with when you went in or how you came out of that situation, that circumstance, that hard place but they were watching how you went through the middle of it. It's in the middle of the fire that people are watching to see can you withstand the heat. I want you to know this today that in the presence of those spectators and naysayers you're coming out on the other side of that fiery furnace and what was meant to kill you couldn't....because of who was in the middle with you. The revelation is in the middle not the beginning or the end! To the natural eye it may look as though I went in and came out alone but it's evident there was somebody in the fire with me. Last year was the year of refining and testing so now come on out and step in to what God has prepared for you. The bible says "I will refine them like silver and test them like gold. They will call on my name and I will answer them; I will say, 'They are my people,' and they will say, 'The LORD is our God" (Zechariah 13:9).

Believe It and Trust the Lord!

26

God Is Still In Control

The bible says that God put Ezekiel in the midst of a valley full of Dry bones....Why? Because He knew that Ezekiel possessed the power to transform that situation. You may be the only Christian in your family, you may be the only Christian on your job, You may be the only Christian on your block or in your neighborhood...But what you need to do is quit pouting and start prophesying. If you're the only believer there it's because God has confidence in you. The Devil is not in charge, I don't care what it looks like, what it feels like or what it sounds like....God is still in control. "The earth is the Lords and the fullness thereof."

This is the time to Arise and Shine...This is the time to stand up and stand out....This is the time to speak the word of God with boldness, authority and power. This is the time that we declare "The devil is a liar...I'm on the eve of the best year of my life." The Good News is The Bad News was WRONG! Believe that and trust the Lord!

Scripture: Proverbs 3:5 "Trust in the LORD with all your heart and lean not on your own understanding."

27

Help Lord, I Have A Problem!

How long are we going to keep going around the same mountain, fighting the same battles, struggling with the same addictions, wrestling with the same fleshly lusts and desires, falling down at the same place over and over again, giving into the same temptations again and again before we are willing to admit we have a problem?

How long are we going to put up with attitudes, addictions, hang-ups, and lusts of the flesh that are self-destructive and in absolute disagreement with the word of God, before we holler..."Help Lord, I have a problem?".

Thus far in life I've learned that the only problem that's unsolvable, unfixable, and incurable, is the one you won't admit to having.

Scripture: Isaiah 40:29-31 "He gives power to the weak and strength to the powerless. Even youths will become weak and tired, and young men will fall in exhaustion. But those who trust in the Lord will find new strength. They will soar high on wings like eagles. They will run and not grow weary. They will walk and not faint.

28

In The Presence Of Thine Enemies

The bible says in Psalms 23:5 "You prepare a table before me in the presence of my enemies. You anoint my head with oil; my cup overflows." Psalms 23 is one of the best known scriptures in the Bible. In it, David speaks in great simplicity and power about the comfort and protection of God. Psalms 23 has provided peace to people going through great distress, loss, pain, jealousy and envy and persecution. The Hebrew word for prepare means to arrange, to set in order, to furnish, to ordain, to lay or to set in a row.

I've been hearing this scripture for several days and as I stopped this morning and took note of the things and people around me I have noticed that this promise is being manifested right now in the lives of God's people. So I encourage you to stop fussing and fighting with people and let God be God. The bible says "Vengeance is mine; I will repay, saith the Lord." God does not need our help…so move out of the way and prepare to sit before the feast that the Lord is preparing for you right now…In the presence of thine enemies.

Believe It and Trust the Lord!

29
Ask God To Change You

There's something wrong if you're still doing the things that you did 5, 10, 15, or 20 years ago. There's something wrong if you attend church or have a relationship with God but nothing in you or your life has changed. There's something wrong if you're in the same position today as you were this time last year. There's something wrong if you don't have a plan, a vision, a dream or a clue. There's something wrong if you know the word but refuse to live it. There's something wrong if God is showing up week after week and everybody's getting delivered and saved but you. Every night before I go to bed I ask God to let me see me how He sees me and then I ask Him to remove everything that's not of Him or like Him...If there's something wrong ask God to help you fix it!

Consider what happens when a caterpillar enters the cocoon, only to emerge later as a butterfly. The caterpillar doesn't change its basic nature. Metamorphosis reveals what was always there in the genes of the caterpillar. Caterpillars can't fly. But they were born to fly. When the caterpillar has been changed into a butterfly, it becomes what God always intended it to be.

Scripture: Romans 12:2 "And do not be conformed to this world, but be transformed by the renewing of your mind, that you may prove what is that good and acceptable and perfect will of God."

30

Where Are The Men of God?

"Where are the Godly men Lord and will I ever get married?" Some of you feel that the chances of a Godly man in the kingdom of God finding you are slim. Sadly, many Christians have not comprehended the fact that we are in the midst of a spiritual war and the church is being fired upon from all angles.....Manhood, marriage and sexual purity are under a vicious assault.

Women of God before you shed another tear because of the unavailability of Godly men in the church, I need you to ponder this: In this war satan has devised a sinister plot to keep all women of God Brokenhearted, Barren, Bewildered and Depressed. Hear the word of the Lord...The devil doesn't want to see any woman of God happily married to a true man of God. Why? Because he knows when that glorious event happens, the born-again, Spirit-filled couple will raise up a godly heritage and he is fighting fiercely to prevent that God-given vision from coming to pass in your life. So Instead of crying tears of sorrow, you should be righteously indignant, (See Ephesians 4:26). Why? Because the devil has no legal right to halt or hinder God's vision for your life, (See Luke 13:16).

Scripture: Exodus 1:15-16;1:22 "And the king of Egypt spoke to the Hebrew midwives, of which the name of the one was Shiphrah, and the name of the other Puah: And he said, When ye do the office of a midwife to the Hebrew women, and see them upon the stools; if it be a son, then ye shall kill him: but if it be a daughter, then she shall live. 22) And Pharaoh charged all his people, saying, Every son that is born ye shall cast into the river, and every daughter ye shall save alive.

Write this down on the tablet of your heart. There is a stirring in the realm of the spirit. We are on the verge of seeing a mass harvest of men come into the Body of Christ, to the likes of which the church has never seen before. The awesome thing about this move of God is — these men won't be carnal-minded, weak in faith or bound by the spirit of religion. These men will be like Joshua, Caleb, Peter and Moses. They will be strong in the spirit. However, in order for this next mighty move of God to take place, the midwives must be strategically positioned at the stools. They will be called SPIRITUAL MIDWIVES. These are the women of God, the Lord has specifically chosen to intercede for the men. These women have a heart after God. They understand the plot of satan to kill the men but let the women live and like their predecessors, they are committed to making the sacrifice. These spiritual midwives will stay at the altar of God and see to it that these men get birthed into the kingdom of God.

Women of God You won't have to cry any more tears because there are no great men of God in the church. The Lord has made you to be a Helpmeet and He will provide for you the desires of your heart: husband, children and a happy and secure home. BUT! You must be willing to sacrifice your time at the altar of God.

31
I'll Wait!

He gave her his all but because she never wanted him... she took what was given but kept what he ultimately desired to herself...her heart. She was the desire of his heart yet he wasn't what she desired at all. So in his pain he turned to drugs, alcohol and women...things he had no desire for. He indulged in the pleasures of the world to keep from admitting that his heart's desire was not the will of God for his life. When he finally woke up he realized that the person he had become was now someone that he didn't even want....all because of his desire.

If he had trusted in the Lord and did good God would have given him what to desire. If he had delighted himself in the Lord and committed his ways unto Him the Lord would have brought that desire to pass.

Tell the next one... I'LL WAIT!

~Pastor Thadeaus Lee~

Scripture: Proverbs 3:5-6 ""Trust in the LORD with all your heart, And lean not on your own understanding; In all your ways acknowledge Him, And He shall direct your paths."

39

Nuggets…On the Path2Life

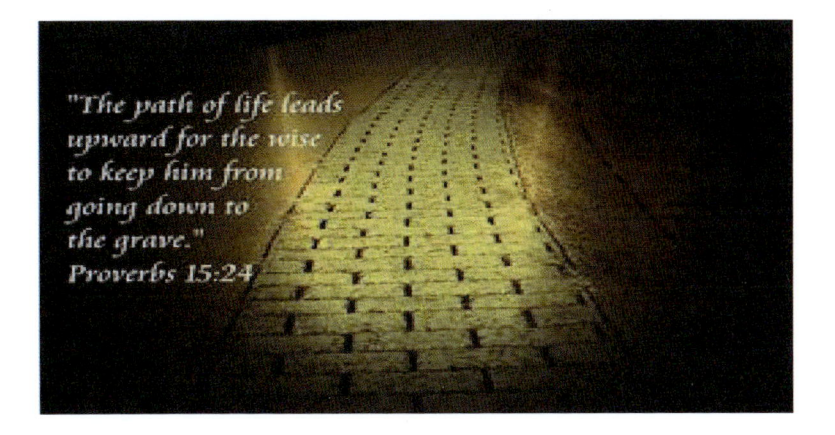

> "The path of life leads upward for the wise to keep him from going down to the grave."
> Proverbs 15:24

1) What you consume (eat) will ultimately determine how much strength and energy you will have on any given day. You will never make it to the finish line (your destined place) or have the strength to make it through the hard times if you're not consuming (eating and being fed) the word of God. There's nothing like a good word (meal) that provides nourishment for the entire week. Having trouble with your strength? Then start eating right!

2) I woke-up with: You can't have 3 without previously obtaining two. The Body of Christ is trying to get the promises without doing what's required to get to the promises (repentance, forgiveness, new heart, sinless life, accepting Jesus and submitting to His will). We can't skip the things we don't want to do and get

right to the good part...NO the Lord is saying you cannot get to three without having completed one and two. If three is your desire then start with one and keep going until you get to the good part....Trust God and Believe His word!

3) Revelation 20:12....."And I saw the dead, small and great, stand before God; and the books were opened: and another book was opened, which is the book of life: and the dead were judged out of those things which were written in the books, according to their works." Men and Women of God, this judgment can be classified as the final judgment because once a man or woman stands before God, and is judged, it's either heaven or hell… there's no turning back. Unlike traffic court, when you appear before this Judge, you get no time extensions to get your act together. There are no provisions for you to file a motion to delay your case. You can't call together a dream team of attorneys such as Mark Geragos and Robert Shapiro to plead your case. If you meet the requirements, you go unto the resurrection of life. If you fail to meet the requirements, you go unto the resurrection of damnation. Oh, but Thank God for Jesus and that we still have breath in our bodies and have been given this moment to repent!

4) "An olive must be crushed to get to the oil inside of it...You're just being crushed so the anointing in you can flow. Crushing feels much like punishment...You're not being punished you're just being processed for the oil that's required for the assignment that's awaiting you!" If God will use you greatly He must first crush you deeply! God cannot use you to any great measure until you've came under and have come through His crushing! Crushing not only cleanses you but it changes you. After wrestling all night the

bible says that Jacob said "I won't let you go until you bless me."

5) When God tells you seven...six won't do. In the bible Naaman was told to dip in the Jordan River seven times...out of obedience he did it and was healed. The Lord told Joshua to have the armed men march around the city once each day, for six days. And On the seventh day to march around the walls of Jericho seven times and on the seventh time around to shout and the walls would fall flat! Out of obedience they did what the Lord said and God did what He promised....the walls fell down. When God tells you seven...six won't do. Out of obedience you have to do what the Lord commands even when it doesn't make sense to you...If you're not willing to do it how God wants it done then don't ask Him why aren't you healed or why aren't you delivered yet. If you're not willing to give Him 7 then don't bother doing 3,4,5,and 6! Obedience is better than sacrifice...Believe and Trust the Lord!

6) Your mouth can keep you in a temporary position permanently...Your life is a result of what's coming out of your mouth so basically what lives in your mouth lives in your future. Therefore, repeat after me...."I'm not broke I'm just in between blessings!"

7) Your praise is a powerful weapon! While you're praising God your enemies are going into mass confusion and beginning to turn on each other. While your praising God, He's fighting for you and positioning you for prosperity. There's a breakthrough in your praise, a poverty breaking and a hell shaking anointing...So don't stop praising cause it's the most powerful weapon that you have. Believe It and Trust the Lord!

8) I don't care what you're facing today...One word from God is all you need. I decree to every person holding this book that in the very same place that the enemy said it was going to end, you're going to step into a new beginning and the greatest blessing of your life. I don't care what you've been told...I don't care what the banker said, the doctor or the lawyer...I want to you to know what the Lord is saying. It doesn't matter what people said, the economy or what the government is saying...I want you to know what the Lord is saying! Is there a word from the Lord? Glad you asked...Yes there is..."God is getting ready to bless you in some unusual ways and He's going to use your enemies to do it. Some of the mean, spiteful, vengeful people that's been trying to destroy you are going to turn around and bless you. From the same place that the enemy was launching his attacks against you, blessings are going to come to you."

9) You may be in the middle of a drought, you may not see any evidence of rain in the sky: But Elijah didn't say he saw, he said he heard: The Sound is your sign that the rain is on its way (everything sounds crazy and nothing is making sense)...But God! It's getting ready to rain, the rain is on its way, I hear the sound of an abundance of rain. That may not mean anything to some of you, but for somebody reading this little nugget of truth it means everything. What does the rain mean? Glad you asked....it means life, recovery restoration, the rivers will run again, fish will be caught again, the crops will grow again,, there will be joy where there has been sorrow, there will be laughter where there has been weeping. It's on the way, it's on the way, it's on the way, it's on the way...Your Help is on the way, Your answer is on the way, Your

breakthrough is on the way. Keep your fight men and women of God and keep your faith, don't give-up now...I hear the sound of an abundance of rain!

10) The bible says "The pharisee said, "God, I thank you because I'm not like these other people. I fast, and I give a tithe, and I do these religious things, and I thank you that I'm not like this dirty tax collector." And the tax collector said, "Be merciful to me a sinner." Jesus said he went home justified."

"For everyone who exalts himself will be humbled, and he who humbles himself will be exalted." Well today the Lord is saying ""If you want my blessing, humble yourself." Somebody was born here in the United States, so he's better than somebody that came from India. Somebody makes $90,000 a year, so he's better than somebody that makes $20,000. Somebody is an executive, so he's better than somebody who is a laborer. Somebody has a college degree, so he's better than somebody that has a high school diploma. Somebody has graduate degrees, so he's better than somebody else. He's a professional person, he's a doctor or lawyer, so he's superior to somebody who doesn't have those skills. Just because you're in the Lexus or Mercedes Benz doesn't make you better than the guy that's in the Chevrolet. A haughty attitude says "I don't need a savior." But humility says, "I must have a Savior." The humility says, "Without the cross, I am lost." I pray this morning that we all understand what humility is and that we will humble ourselves before the Lord and acknowledge our dependence on the Lord!

11) The day that you hear the Word of God is the most important day of your life. The Word is the Power of God, Your healing is in the Word

,Your deliverance and joy is in the Word, and so is your Prosperity, anointing and destiny. The bible says "In the beginning was the Word, the Word was with God and the Word was God, the same was in the beginning with God, all things were made by him (The Word) and without him (The Word) was not anything made that was made" (John 1:1-3). Everything begins with the Word. You can shout, dance, run, holler, talk in tongues and jump pews, but you haven't even got started until you get in the Word. Faith is the hand that reaches out and takes hold of the blessings of God, but it's the Word of God that quickens the hand of faith. "Stretch forth thy hand" was Jesus command to the man with the withered hand, and at his word faith came alive. So today I say to you, "Stretch forth thy hand and grab a hold of the word of God because that's where your promise lives."Believe It and Trust God!

12) What qualifies as Nineveh today? Nineveh is whatever pulls you out of your comfort zone…..Nineveh is the place God calls where you don't want to go…..Nineveh is the people who have hurt you deeply and God says, "Go and give them my message." Nineveh is danger. Nineveh is discomfort. Nineveh is whatever you hate that God loves deeply. The bible says "But Jonah ran away from the LORD and headed for Tarshish. He went down to Joppa, where he found a ship bound for that port. After paying the fare, he went aboard and sailed for Tarshish to flee from the LORD." God said, "Go east." Jonah said, "I'm going west."

If you look at the scripture you'll see that Jonah went "down" four times:

He went "down" to Joppa (v. 3).

He went "down" into the hold of the ship (v. 4).

He went "down" into the sea (v. 15).

He went "down" into the belly of the great fish (v. 17).

That's not a coincidence. It's a statement about what happens when we disobey God's call. Any time you run from God, you never go "up"; you always go "down."

When we decide to disobey God, there is always a boat going to Tarshish…..And there is always room for one more passenger. When we decide to run from the Lord, Satan is happy to provide the transportation. Jonah was God's man for Nineveh! And whether he wanted to go or not....He was going! And the same goes for you Fam...so go ahead and tell God yes and save yourself some trouble! You say, "I don't want to go." God says, "I'll just make you willing to go.

13) "Everyone is carrying some emotional baggage and everyone struggles to keep it hidden. A lot of us are walking around with bags of smelly inner garbage that we choose to ignore simply because we've packed our garbage in expensive name brand luggage. We're weighed down with trash on the inside and try to cover it up by superficial means... having the bomb.com hair….nails….make-up….clothes….purses and shoes.

Hiding our issues doesn't make them go away and dressing them up doesn't make them look good. Trash is trash and it stinks! It's time to relieve ourselves of all the baggage in our life once and for all!

"The first official stop on this voyage back to YOU is baggage check-in…..You'll need to drop off any unnecessary baggage you're carrying. You know…those bags of hurt, disappointment, mistakes, failures, and sins that you have lugged around with you and that have caused you to stay in a place of torment. The ones you've taken in and out of relationship after relationship. You know… those secrets, fears, and unfulfilled promises that you can't get off your mind that weigh you down and prevent you from moving forward.

It's time to relieve yourself of them once and for alll. You won't need them where you're going! The truth of the matter is, you should have never had them in the first place, but life happened and you have bags to prove it." Cast your cares on the LORD and he will sustain you; he will never let the righteous fall."

14) What has God promised us? The Promise Land...It's a place of happiness, a place of blessing, a place of peace. It's what the book of Hebrews calls "entering God's rest." This is a place where you feel good about your life, you find satisfaction in your work, you experience joy in your relationships, and you're relaxed about your financial situation. This is the life that God desires for his people -- a life of contentment.
Haven't gotten there yet? Take a look at who's wandering in the wilderness with you...Your blessing, Your Promise, and Your Destined Place is being held up because of who you're wandering around with. What should have taken you a few days have and will take you 40 years. Catch the wisdom in this and Believe It!

15) What you allow in your life will ultimately begin to rule over you. You lose pieces of yourself with every compromise that you make....suddenly you are no longer who you were but who and what this person, place or thing has created. Your associations are a reflection...a mirror image of who you really are. Sadly, you're the last one to see the image you're portraying to the world. There are things in your life that aren't supposed to be there....they were sent to harm you, discredit you and to kill you. The alarm has been sounded, God has sent a warning...Open your eyes and see what's in your presence and open your ears and hear what thus says the Lord about your present condition." I hear the sound of pigs squealing and it's high pitched and loud...they're excited about the new meat that's been thrown in their pen. Lord help us right now in the name of Jesus!

16) The truth of the matter is...You haven't seen God's best! If you're living in accordance to His word and have applied the laws, statutes, and commandments to your life then this message is for YOU. What's coming your way is about to blow your mind...you think you've had some good things and have experienced some good times but you haven't seen anything yet....You are on the eve of receiving His best. To those who have chosen to live in mess and go about things their way...don't you dare be mad at those who are about to receive this blessing. Repent and give your life to God and leave the foolish things of this world alone...I see two lines of people: The Included and The Excluded. Which line will you be in? Your sin isn't worth you missing out on this great move of God.

17) It's true that one of the keys to life and good relationships is effective communication. And for effective communication to occur, there must be effective listening. This is true not only in developing relationships with one another, but in our relationship with God as well. Why do we study the Bible? Why do we pray? Why do we worship? The process looks something like this:

COMMUNICATION: Listening to God

COMPREHENSION: Understanding what God says

CONFIDENCE: Trusting in what God says

CHANGE: Being transformed by what God says

Without this process of communication, there simply cannot be any real spiritual change in the life of man. Because of this, God is deeply concerned about how well we listen when we are listening. The bible says "Take care then how you hear, for to the one who has, more will be given, and from the one who has not, even what he thinks that he has will be taken away."

18) What have you been saying? The bible says "Death and life are in the power of the tongue: and they that love it shall eat the fruit thereof." Your life is a reflection of what you've been speaking. Who I am today is what I spoke yesterday...What I'll be tomorrow will be a result of what I spoke today. What have you been saying about you?

It's a tremendous disappointment to the heart of God, that there are so many who will never fulfill their destiny. Your destiny is not up to God and it's not up to the devil....God has already predetermined what He desires for your life...Now it's up to you to set your course for your destiny....by saying about yourself what God has already said about you. Then and only then will you find yourself moving quickly in the direction of your destined place.

19) There are times in life when you'll feel like you're headed down a one way street in the wrong direction but don't stop moving...what looks like the wrong direction to you is the right direction to God...the bible says "Trust in the LORD with all thy heart and lean not to thy own understanding." It's during these times on your journey that you'll have the desire to stop and ask for directions...from friends and family and from anybody who will give you a prophetic word. But the Lord wants you to know today that your blueprint, your map, and your directions are in His hands...Are you tired of wandering? Then stop asking everybody but God are you headed in the right direction. The enemy enjoys sending you around in circles and on a wild goose chase....Believe It and Trust God!

20) The enemy is closer than you think....he's in most of your conversations, in your circle of friends, and around just about every corner. Know those who labor among you, says the Lord. There are many people who don't even know that they're being used...but if you open your eyes

and ears (discernment) you'll know before they do. The enemy is in your camp...will you pack up your tent and leave where God has planted you or will you use the authority that God has given you and make it leave? Guard your conversations, says the Lord...you're being probed (To seek to uncover information about someone or something)!

21) The people around you will never understand your praise...so stop trying to explain. They'll never understand where He's taking you because they really don't know where He brought you from....stop trying to explain. They will never understand the open doors and the favor because instead of watching they're trying to run through with you...stop trying to explain and keep on running. You know what God has done for you, You know what God has brought you through, You know why the doors are open and the favor is resting upon your life....so just keep praising and stop trying to explain. What God has for you is for you so there's no need to explain anything...Believe That!

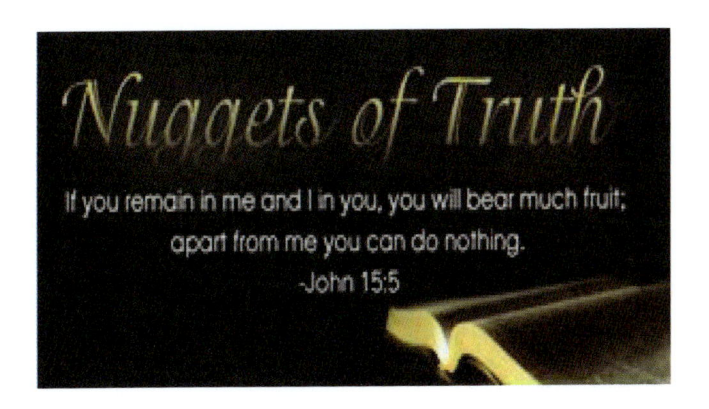

Nuggets of Truth

If you remain in me and I in you, you will bear much fruit; apart from me you can do nothing.
-John 15:5

Pastor Patty

Stop allowing people to show up in your life and they're not showing up in their own!

Revelations from My Father

Books by Pastor Patty

Available on amazon.com

and

http://www.etsy.com/shop/TheCrushedOlive

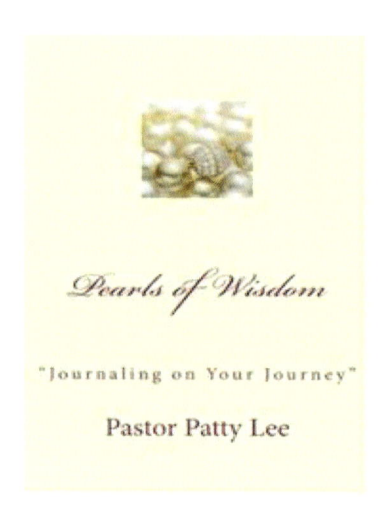

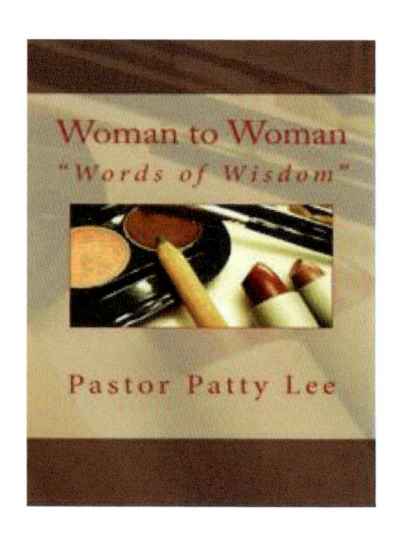

Revelations from My Father

Printed in Great Britain
by Amazon